A PRACTICAL PATTERN MANUAL
FOR WOODCARVING AND OTHER CRAFTS

BOOK I

Timber Press
Portland, Oregon
1981

A Practical Pattern Manual for Woodcarving and Other Crafts
Art McKellips

© Copyright 1981 by Timber Press

LIBRARY OF CONGRESS CATALOGING
IN PUBLICATION DATA:

ISBN 0-917304-67-5

Timber Press
P.O. Box 1632
Beaverton, OR 97075
USA

PRINTED IN THE UNITED STATES OF AMERICA

Table of Contents

IV

Introduction

      A couple of years ago I wrote a book to introduce the novice to the art of woodcarving (*Woodcarving For Beginners,* Timber Press, 1977). In it I tried to explain the basics of this art. I promised further books at the time and this is the first of those. This is a pattern book with 26 patterns for cut-out, bas relief and figure-in-the-round pieces. I have provided drawn patterns with photographs of some of the finished carvings. In addition, there is background information on each figure as well as recommendations as to the kind of wood and tools to be used and carving information. For further assistance you can refer to my first book. These two books, along with wood, tools and some work space should provide all you need for many hours of happy carving and the satisfaction of filling your home with beautiful pieces that will impress your friends, family and, most importantly, you.

Cheerful Chiseling,
Art

How to Use This Book

This is a book of patterns designed especially for woodcarving. It will allow those of you who cannot draw, who want further experience before designing your own projects, or simply need some new ideas, to select a pattern and give it a try. This is not a how-to book, and I cannot be there with you, looking over your shoulder and answering your every question. I have tried to pass on some advice and tips regarding the patterns presented here, but it is not possible to lead you step by step through each carving. I did that for you in my book *Woodcarving for Beginners.* The basic principles you learned there will guide you on these patterns as well.

All the pattern pages are blank on the back so that they can be torn out of the book if you want to. Also, a set of grids has been provided if you want to enlarge or reduce any of the patterns. How to use a grid is explained in my first book.

The recommended tool list for each project is just that, a recommendation. If you started carving with *Woodcarving for Beginners* you know which tools are your favorites by now, and what you can make them do. Perhaps you've even started a carving tool collection, if so, by all means use it. Others will do equally well as ones I would use for any specific pattern.

The same holds true for wood choice. I have made suggestions, but you may have some available that will do a great job for you. Use it by all means, you are not required to use what I recommend.

A word also about "type of carving" listed here. There are basically only two types, either bas relief, or a statue in the round. Every carving will fit one or the other classification. Within the category of relief carvings there are different styles. Some are carved into rectangular boards, some cut out of boards, and some so thick that they go three-quarters of the way around the figure. They are all relief carvings, however, unless they go all the way around the figure, completely freeing it of any background; this is a statue in the round.

Nearly every pattern can be done in a number of different types of bas relief, depending on how much work you choose to make of it and the type of wood you have available for the purpose. The simplest is to carve the subject onto a board, either leaving a raised border, or setting the ground down all the way around, leaving only the subject raised out and rounded. A cut out design, where the subject is cut free of the background in spots, thus incorporating negative space which forms an important part of the design, is far more challenging and in many cases far more attractive, but it is a matter of personal taste.

Most of the patterns presented here are similar to ones I have used at some time in my work over the past twenty years. Many are drawn from memory since the original carving has long since been purchased and left my hands. Unfortunately, no photos exist for some, so for these you will have to rely solely on the experience you have gained so far and the pattern drawing for reference. If you have done the patterns in *Woodcarving for*

Beginners, these will add to that experience because some are very easy and others are far more difficult. You will learn something with each carving you do, regardless of its difficulty, and sometimes you learn the most when you tax your abilities to the limit.

Just as with the selection of tools and wood, by necessity the finishing of your piece is left up to you. You may like wax, or commercial products like Danish Oil or Deft. Use what pleases you, after all I'm not interested in seeing my work cloned, merely in providing you with the basics to develop your own style from.

Cheerful Chiseling,
Art

VII

Lion's Head

I. "The King of Beasts" may be an exaggeration, but this ferocious looking fellow has been the subject of artists for centuries. He often appeared on heraldic shields and the emblems of medieval knights as a symbol of ferocity and strength. In fact it is the female who does most of the work of hunting to keep his majesty well fed, but she lacks the impressive mane, so it is the male that is depicted in art work. He may be lazy by nature, but he can be fierce indeed when provoked.

1

II. Type of Carving

A very shallow relief carving, done with simple line-drawing type V-cuts in a rectangular board and recessed shallowly into the board.

III. Materials

A. Tools

1. V-tools: ⅛", ¼", ½"
2. Gouges: ¼" #4, ½" #4
3. Chisels: ½" #1
4. Knife
5. Mallet

B. Wood
Basswood, Julutong or Pine, 1" × 11¼" × 13".

IV. Directions for Carving

A. Strap the carving to a work table top so it does not slide around.
B. Transfer the pattern to the wood.
C. Use the ½" V-tool around the face from the hairline to the chin whiskers. Do not cut too close to the chin whiskers; put them in with smaller tools.
D. Use knife tip to put in the mane down from the side of the face.
E. Use ¼" V and ½" V to put in the mane that starts above the ears. Slant the mane down so that the ears are left raised out. Turn your ½" #4 on its side and use the wing tips to create the strands of the mane. The slanted cut will leave one edge high and the bottom low to reflect the strands of the hair.
F. Use the ¼" V to put in the lines on the flat surface of the face. Cutting straight in with the V will give a thin line; rolling the tool on its side will create a widened line. The face is simply a shallow relief line drawing, but the depth you give the mane will frame it to good effect.

V. Finishing

  A. Sand carving smooth.

  B. Stain with commercial stain to desired color.

  C. Let dry and buff with clear shoe polish for soft luster, or apply commercial wood sealer in semi-gloss.

2

Scottish Warrior

I. The unique garb of this figure makes him immediately recognizable as a representative of the Highlands of Scotland, and the detailing in his costume permits the carver to add many of his own touches in scabbard and hilt shape, plaid pattern, etc.

II. Type of Carving

Statue in the round.

III. Materials

A. Tools

1. V-tools: ⅛″, ¼″, ½″
2. Gouges: ⅛″ #6, ⅛″ #11, ¼″ #4, ½″ #4, ⅝″ #11, ⅝″ #5
3. Chisels or skew chisels: ¼″, ½″
4. Knife
5. Mallet
6. Deer Antler

B. Wood

Block of basswood, 17″ × 3½″ × 5″.

IV. Directions for Carving

A. Bandsaw out the figure, both side profile and front view.

    1. You will not have to use a cradle if you lay the figure on its back to cut the front view. It is flat along the scabbard and the point between the shoulders will ride evenly on the saw table so your blade will not bind up.

    2. Leave at least ¼″ of extra stock on the back of the head when bandsawing along your pencil line, otherwise there will not be enough woodstock left to finish off the back of the head. The head is turned to the side in this carving and the difference between your two-dimensional pattern and the three-dimensional finished carving will be nearly ¼″.

    3. Do not bandsaw up under the elbow of the left arm since the same dimensional problem occurs there. It looks right, but does not transfer the way the sketch looks. Bandsaw straight in to the body and cut out the waste by hand tool after establishing the position of the forearm. Do the same where the left hand lies on the breast, otherwise the arm may appear too short.

    B. Clamp the statue base into the vise.

    C. Set in the raised forearm stop cuts first and slant it back to the elbow.

Be sure that the angle of the upper arm, from shoulder to elbow corresponds to the pattern so the forearm slant will be right.

> D. Drill two holes, front to back, between the legs, one below the scabbard and one above. This will permit you to get tools in for shaping the legs and scabbard. Leave the legs until last so you'll have enough strength in the wood to pound on upper block with mallet.

> E. Draw a line to set the nose and the center of the face over the top of the head and down the face so you have the proper angle for the turned head. Set in the bonnet with stop cuts. Shape the head up to the bonnet, leaving the bridge protruding to establish face lines back from nose. Define jaw with #11 and trim the neck back in. Stop cut with small V up along neck at collar to raise collar up off neck.

> F. Use measurements to finish off shoulder width and waist front and back. Use #4 on edge to cut negative space between arm hanging down and the side of the body. This is done after the arm has been shaped, so there is not much stock to clear.

> G. Take measurement of your scabbard so you know the length to make the blade that is inserted into the basket hilt of the broadsword.

> H. Carve in the belt, sporran and dirk with V-tool and #4 gouge.

> I. Choose the plaid clan pattern of your preference and carve it into the kilt with the knife tip forming the lines. The photograph is of the McDonnell of Keppoch and the clan badge is carved in the base.

> J. Remove the waste wood between the scabbard and the right leg, followed by the waste below the scabbard. Do this back to front so you don't destroy the scabbard.

> K. Shape the rear leg first by turning it so the left leg faces you, then reverse the process, turning the statue to do the right leg.

> L. Insert the sword blade into the basket hilt. Peg the shield onto the forearm with a dowel and sharpen the protrusion into a spike.

V. Finishing

> A. Sand lightly and use a deer antler to smooth the grain.
> B. Stain and wipe.
> C. Apply clear shoe polish and buff with a shoe brush.

6

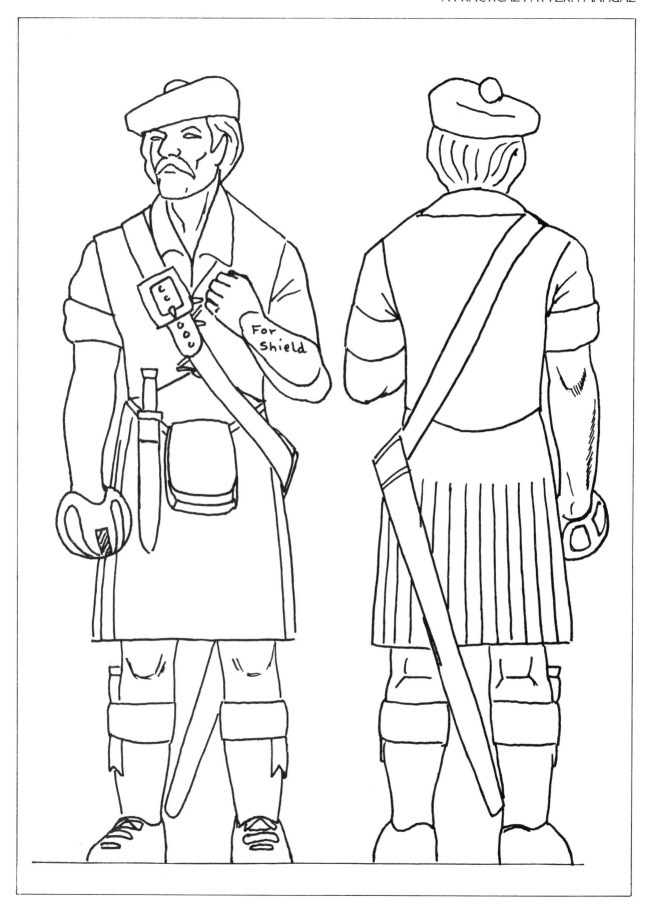

Shield

Spike in center

Dowel

Side view of shield with Spike used for Close in fighting

The Caveman

I. This figure was carved to represent the idea that true progress is a spiritually motivated state of mind, not just technological advancement. The caveman's club could fell only one at a time, our modern weapons could wipe out humanity, but the mentality behind both is the same.

II. Type of Carving

Statute in the round.

III. Materials

A. Tools

1. V-tools: ⅛″, ¼″
2. Gouges: ⅛″ #6, ⅛″ #11, ¼″ #4, ½″ #4, ⅝″ #11
3. Chisels or skew chisels: ¼″, ½″
4. Knife
5. Mallet
6. Deer Antler

B. Wood
Block of basswood, 14″ × 3½″ × 4″.

IV. Carving Directions

A. Since there are no protruding limbs bandsaw out profile shape.

B. Clamp firmly in a bench vise.

C. Drill holes, front to back, between legs to assist in removing waste.

D. Set in the arms on the sides with either V-tools or #11 veiner.

E. Set in beard back to shoulders and to fall of hair, then set nose to find the most prominent point.

F. Use knife and smaller gouges and V-tools to shape features and musculature above the waist. Use the #4s to give the body a broad, flat, slab-like muscle structure.

G. Use ⅛″ #11 to put in the ribs.

H. Use ⅛″ V for hair strands on beard and hair.

I. Turn #4 on edge and go straight through between sides and arms. Clean out with knife.

J. Clean out and shape opening between legs and feet.

K. Shape loin cloth with V-tools and #4s.

L. Detail leg and foot muscle structure with ⅛″ V and ⅛″ #11.

M. Drill hole through hand. Carve and insert club.

V. Finishing

A. Sand smooth, compress surface vigorously with a deer antler.

B. Stain and wipe.

C. Apply shoe polish and buff with shoe brush.

12

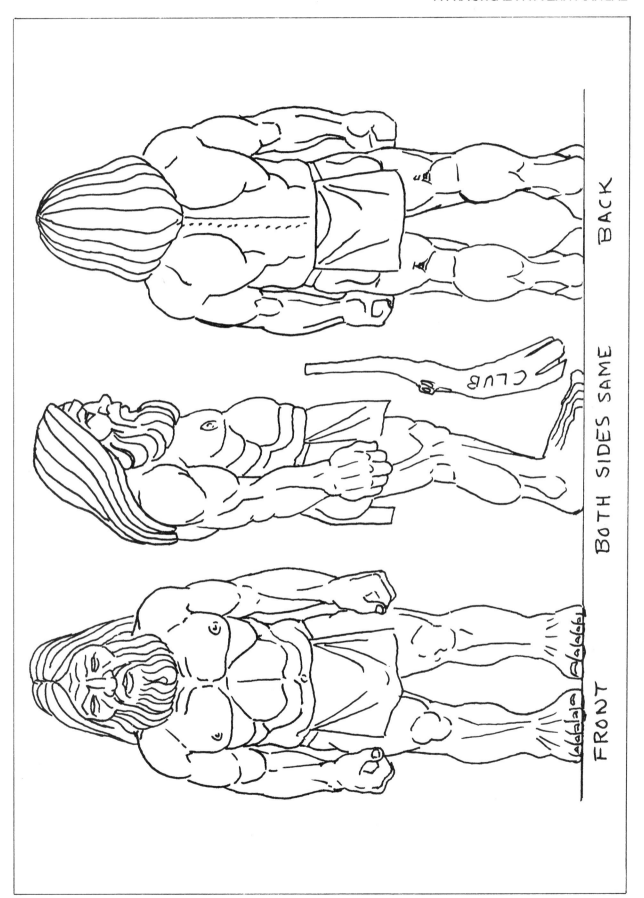

Greek Warrior

I. The warrior of Alexander the Great's time was heralded as a fierce fighting man. His distinctive armor could not be confused with that of any other culture. Here his heavy bronze helmet is tipped up to enable him to see and hear better. He wears a leather jerkin for modesty, not protection, as his other body armament was bronze legshields form-fitted to his calves, and he depended primarily on his shield to protect his torso. The shield size shown in the pattern is very small, but some of the shields were huge cumbersome affairs. I suggest that you carve the shield to the size you desire. The sword is a carved insert.

II. Type of Carving

A statue in the round.

III. Materials

A. Tools

1. V-tools: ⅛″, ¼″, ½″
2. Gouges: ⅛″ #6, ⅛″ #11, ¼″ #4, ½″ #4, ¼″ #11
3. Chisels or skew chisels: ⅛″, ¼″
4. Knife
5. Mallet
6. Deer Antler

B. Wood
Block of basswood, 12″ × 3″ × 3″.

IV. Directions for Carving

A. Before trying this one I would hope that you have gained some statue experience on the Cowboy and Sea Captain figures. The techniques for this one are similar, but the features are more realistically defined, and so more detailed

1. Cut out profile on a bandsaw and retain the back piece to use as a cradle to lay the figure back in on. Draw on the front view. Lay the piece in the back piece cradle and saw out the front view. In effect you have cut away waste on the front and back and both sides now.

B. Clamp 3″ base in vise.

C. Shape both arms, giving body size consideration as you set in your stop cuts. Remove waste and measure across stomach and chest. Remove waste to the proper measurements, front and rear.

D. Use ½″ V or #11 to shape horsehair plume and round helmet leaving the upraised plume.

E. Carefully measure and draw on face. Work slants back from nose to ears and hair. Work in neck to measurements. Use small tools on the confined spaces as well as features and eye hole in helmet.

F. Work in legs, using knife tip to get in between calves and ankles.

G. Carve sword and shield and apply to finished statue.

V. Finishing

A. Sand any spots which need it. Apply deer antler to compress the grain, but not on the horse hair plume, it might break off if too thin.

B. Stain and wipe.

C. Buff with shoe polish and shoe brush.

16

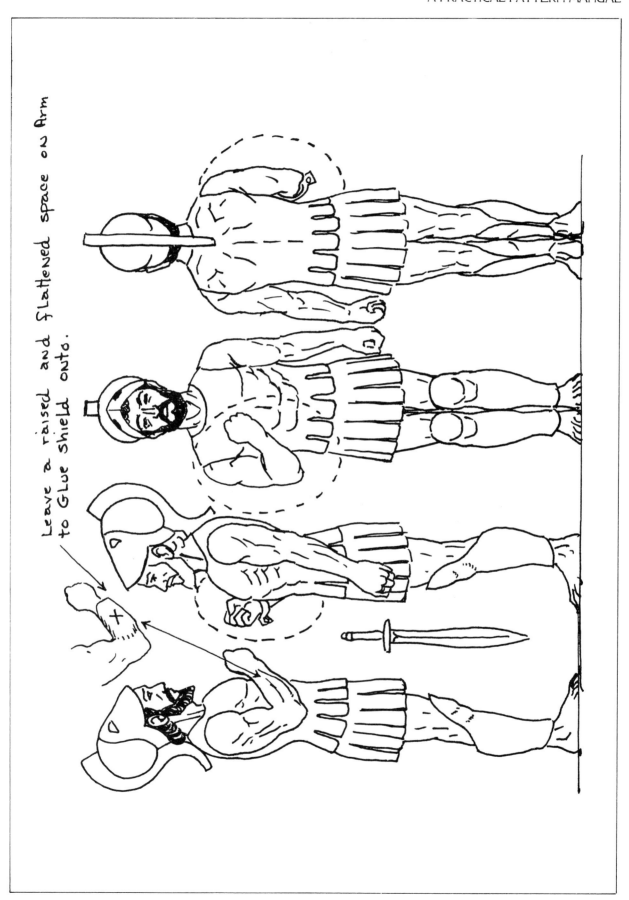

Sea Captain

I. Seamen have been a popular woodcarving subject for many years. The seaman, with his distinctive garb, has been a familiar figure in many of our population centers since the founding of this country. This figure is very similar in principle to the Cowboy, so the carving directions are the same, with the exception of the hat. The seaman figure is the one used as an example in my first book *Woodcarving for Beginners* and is detailed completely in the chapter on how to carve statues.

II. Type of Carving

A statue in the round.

III. Materials

A. Tools

1. V-tools: ⅛″, ¼″
2. Gouges: ⅛″ #6, ⅛″ #8, ⅜″ #8, ¼″ #4, ½″ #4, ⅜″ #6, ¼″ #6, ⅝″ #11
3. Chisels or skew chisels: ⅛″, ¼″
4. Knife
5. Mallet
6. Deer Antler
7. Bench screw or bench vise

B. Wood

Block of basswood, 14″ × 3½″ × 4″. This allows a 4″ base to clamp firmly in vise or be attached to bench by bench screw to prevent movement while carving.

IV. Directions for Carving

A. Open *Woodcarving for Beginners* to page 44.
B. Bandsaw out profile shape.
C. Clamp base in vise on table.
D. Drill holes between legs to permit waste removal.
E. Set in your stop cuts on sides along arms and around beard and at the bottom of the coat.
F. Block out face and establish nose and ears as these are the highest points, along with the beard on the jaw.
G. Shape face by leaving nose and jaw prominent and sloping cheeks back to ears. Use #4s and smaller gouges as well as the knife to work in the features.
H. Shape hat brim and round crown.
I. Shape the arms, shoulders and jacket both front and back. Buttons can be set round with the gouge tips.

J. Finish off bow legs and feet

V. Finishing

A. Sand smooth any rough spots, work subject over with pressure from
the deer antler.

B. Stain and wipe.

C. Apply clear shoe polish and buff with a shoe brush.

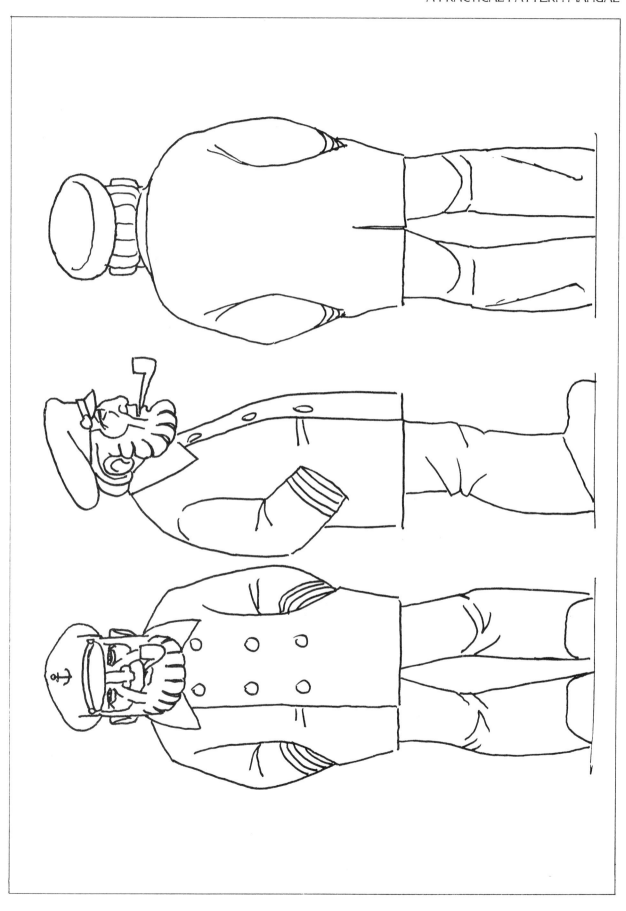

Cowboy

I. The cowboy is an instantly recognizable piece of Americana. His distinctive apparel and rough-hewn features make him an ideal wood carving subject.

II. Typing of Carving

Statue in the round.

III. Materials

A. Tools

1. V-tools: ⅛″, ¼″.
2. Gouges: ⅛″ #6, ⅛″ #8, ⅜″ #8, ¼″ #4, ½″ #4, ⅜″ #6, ¼″ #6, ⅝″ #11.
3. Chisels or skew chisels: ⅛″, ¼″.
4. Knife
5. Mallet
6. Deer Antler
7. Bench screw or bench vise

B. Wood

Block of basswood 14″ × 3½″ × 4″. This is sufficient stock to allow a base about 3¾″ high so you have something to grip firmly while carving.

23

IV. Directions for Carving

A. Bandsaw out a profile of your pattern.

B. Clamp your figure in a bench vise so it will be held firmly as you work.

C. Drill holes between legs to allow easy removal of waste with gouge and knife.

D. Set in your stop cuts on sides along arms and around face, neckerchief and bottom of vest.

E. Trim head back to rounded block form under hat brim with #11 veiner or ½″ V. Shape brim, top and bottom. Leave face blocked out until you establish the position of the nose and ears which are the most prominent guide points.

F. Shape the face by leaving nose and jaw prominent and sloping cheeks back to ears. Use #4s and smaller gouges as well as knife to work in the features.

G. Shape the arms and shoulders, then the torso.

H. Finish off with legs and boots.

V. Finishing

A. Sand over any rough spots. Work the subject over with pressure from the deer antler.

B. Stain and wipe.

C. Apply clear shoe polish and buff with a shoe brush.

24

Heavenly Kingdom

I. This carving is completely symbolic. The cross and the intertwined thorns represent Christ, who died upon the cross while wearing a crown of thorns. The endless circle represents God, and the crown upon the circle the kingdom of heaven. The uncovered hand of peace is grasping the sword, a weapon of war held firmly by the mailed fist, and breaking it against the cross.

Woodcarvers often turn their talents to spiritual carvings. Perhaps it is the fact that wood is a living substance, or perhaps it is that it is an inexpensive medium and so available to the poor, who often lean to the spiritual. Whatever the reason, I believe that this piece is in the mainstream of old carving tradition.

II. Type of Carving

This is a relief cut-out carving and looks best in 1″ wood to keep it light and airy looking.

III. Materials

A. Tools

1. V-tools: ⅛″, ¼″, ½″ or ⅝″
2. Gouges: ⅛″ #6, ¼″ #4, ½″ #4, ⅜″ #6, ¾″ #5, ¼″ #13, ½″ #13
3. Chisels: ½″ #1
4. Knife
5. Mallet
6. Drill, to pierce holes
7. Coping saw, to cut away waste

B. Wood
Basswood or pine, 1″ × 8¼″ × 16″.

IV. Carving

A. In drawing up your pattern to transfer to the wood I would suggest that you slide the broken sword down the base of the cross so as to leave the broken edges just inside the circle. Due to size limitations of the pattern drawing I found it necessary to draw it somewhat higher to meet the size scale, but I assure you it will be a simple and more pleasing presentation when lowered on the cross.

1. Transfer your pattern to the wood.
2. Use your drill to pierce the holes in the waste pieces of wood, such as inside the circle.

3. Insert the coping saw blade through the holes and very carefully cut away the waste pieces.

4. Use either a coping saw or a band saw and carefully cut around the entire exterior of the pattern, freeing it completely from the board.

5. Select a piece of scrap plywood slightly larger than the cut out pattern. Coat the flat surface of the plywood with a white glue, such as Elmer's carpenter glue, and press a single sheet of newspaper down on the glue. Then coat the back of the cut-out with glue and press it down onto the paper surface. While drying the glue will penetrate the paper, bonding the carving through the paper to the plywood. With this for strength, you can pound with a mallet and chisel and protrusions will not break off. When the carving is complete you simply insert a wide, flat chisel under the carving, into the paper level of glue and, twisting the chisel, spring the carving loose. Once dried the carving will not separate from the board without this prying, twisting action.

6. When the glue is dry clamp your board onto a suitable work table.

B. Commence the Carving

1. Set in the deepest points by ½″ V-tool stop lines around the cross, hands and sword and under the rim of the crown. Remember, the circle tilts out higher, over the cross, at the top and slants down to go behind the cross at the bottom, so it is not a flat ground. It will be recessed about ⅜″ deep at the top and a full ⅝″ to ¾″ at the bottom, depending on the total thickness of your board. A circle of ¼″ thick from the back of the board is plenty.

2. Set your high points as the knuckles of the hands and the broken sword ends. Skim the top bars of the cross, slanted down, to a depth of ⅛″ below these high points.

3. The cross shaft slants down in towards the bottom until it allows the thorn crown to stand out, flush with the surface, ¼″ to ⅜″. This slant will be your guide for slanting the wrists down into the thorns. Keep the heel of the hand as a high point, flush with the surface.

4. The detail work on the fingers can be done with ¼″ V, ⅛″ V and ⅛″ #6 and ¼″ #4. The rivets on the mailed fist can be put in with the knife tip, or use a semi-circular gouge to fit the size rivet head you desire. Even a ⅛″ V will incise a circular cut.

5. The crown should be flush at the top in an overhang, and slant back towards the stop cut making a rim at the bottom. Stop cut around the jewels first, then slant off the waste with #4 gouges.

6. Round the vines with flattened thorns to complete your carving.

V. Finishing

A. Sand smooth with sandpaper, going with the grain.

B. Polish with antler.

C. Then, pry loose from the retaining board.

D. I do not recommend staining this light colored wood. I do recommend coating it with oil and buffing in clear shoe polish as a finish. This will tan it, almost as if it had aged for years, but it will remain light colored. Rub on the neutral shoe polish with a rag and buff it vigorously with a shoe brush. It takes several coats to build up the luster.

Grace In Motion

I. This design portrays abstract forms, both human and animal, in graceful fluid movement. The features are kept simple since any detailing would detract from the emphasis on movement. Both forms, although different in structure, typify the beauty found in nature.

II. Type of Carving
Bas relief

III. Materials

A. Tools

1. V-Tools: ⅛″, ¼″, ½″
2. Gouges: ⅜″ #8, ⅜″ #6, ¼″ #13, ¼″ #4, ½″ #4
3. Chisels: ½″ #1
4. Mallet

B. Wood

I suggest walnut which will show considerable "figure" or grain, contributing to the feeling of movement. Recommended size is 1″ × 12″ × 16″. The grain should run vertically.

IV. Carving

A. Strap the walnut down firmly to a bench top carving area. Trace your pattern on with carbon paper. If your pattern lines are difficult to see due to the darkness of the wood go over your design with a white pencil.

B. Outline your figures with a ½″ V stop cut. Do not cut across the impala's body with the ½″ V where the bodies merge. Switch to a smaller V there as you do not wish to "set in" the stop cut the full depth through the impala's body.

C. Boost out the waste up to the stop cuts, setting the "ground" or background depth and leaving the figures raised up from the ground.

D. Set in shallower V cuts along the raised figures to divide off the sections of the torsos. Once you have these sections defined use the flatter gouges to slant in against these cuts, giving the proper twist to the bodies. The surfaces are best shown off with a broad flat stroke. The deeper slanted strokes are used primarily around the outer edges.

E. A ⅜″ #6 will be useful for smooth, hollowed-out areas, such as the flowing hair and under the jaw line. The chisels, when used flat in a pushing stroke, will smooth the surfaces down flat. In using the chisel so that the heel slides across the wood, it will have a tendancy to rise out of the wood, and not smooth too effectively. So experiment with turning your chisel over with the heel upwards on your push stroke. Use care, however, as it will bite in rapidly with the smoothing action and you don't want to go in too deep.

V. Finishing

A. Walnut is a hardwood and the grain lends itself to a very smooth surface. Sand first, going with the grain, with a coarse sandpaper, smoothing down rough edges, but do not grind off areas like the jawline or breasts on the subjects. Next use a fine grit sandpaper and, again, sand with the grain. The final smoothing step can be with a deer antler, bone, or even a tool handle used as an instrument to press down the grain. Go over the entire surface, compressing the grain and polishing it smooth.

B. The finish of walnut lends itself well to spray lacquer, Deft wood filler or a handrubbed finish of linseed oil or a penetrating oil like Danish oil. A true gloss, while undesirable on most woods, can be used on this piece, however I prefer a semi-gloss as opposed to the wood trophy high gloss finish.

32

Grace — abstract forms in motion

The Truth Shall Make You Free

I. This symbolic design is based on the concept that truth and knowledge will break the shackles of ignorance and permit enlightenment with the blessing of the Holy Spirit, as symbolized by the circle. The lamp, here held aloft by the hand, has long stood as a symbol of learning.

II.Type of Carving

The pattern is intended here for use in a bas relief piece carved from a plank. However, as with many patterns, it could be rendered as a statue in the round. My original was carved into half a log of walnut.

III. Materials

A. Tools

Your choice of depth to ground the background will dictate part of this. Should your choice be shallow relief line carving use 1″ thick wood and a ¼″ V-tool to carve it in. If you choose to do it in a deeper relief form use a 2″ thick board with a ½″ V-tool to stop cut your pattern. If you wish to scale this pattern either up or down in size refer to that section in my book *Woodcarving for Beginners.*

B. For the deeper relief you will need

1. V-Tools: ½″, ⅛″, ¼″
2. Gouges: ¼″ #4, ½″ #4, ⅜″ #8, ¾″ #6
3. Chisels: ½″ #1
4. Knife
5. Mallet

C. Wood

Use basswood, pine, mahogany, or julutong, 2″ × 10″ × 17″ with the grain running vertically. Any tight-grained wood will be suitable, since this carving has a minimum of fine detail and a visible grain will not conflict with the boldness of the carved form.

IV. Carving

A. Set in your outlining stop cut around the figure with the ½″ V down to the circle. At the portion of the legs, which cross the circle, either cut more shallowly, or use the ¼″ V as you do not wish to force the circle depth down to the rest of the background depth.

Pay particular attention to the depth of your cross-grain stop cut around the chain and be sure that it is deep enough to boost out the background waste with the larger gouge without raising off or breaking loose the chain from the background. Once the background is set to depth set the flat surface of the circle about ¼″ above the ground. The figure itself is surfaced with slanted cuts, and has no absolutely flat surfaces. Experiment as you slant your gouge from the center of the left leg to the back stop cut. Since this leg is forward and most prominent, it is important that you find the correct gradual slant. Too steep a slant will force you to set the background deeper as you will widen the figure considerably. A shallow slant is best to test for proportions.

36

The tip of the knife, as well as the extreme edge of the chisel, can help you in shaping the chain links. The inverted chisel will help you smooth the carved surface and compressing the grain by rubbing vigorously with a deer antler will give a nice final effect. Compressing the grain with the antler can also help accentuate any muscles or tendons which you wish to make more prominent.

V. Finishing

A. In soft woods use a commercial stain, followed by clear shoe polish or a Deft wood sealer in semi-gloss.

B. In hardwoods rub in an oil, such as linseed oil or Danish oil, and buff with clear shoe polish.

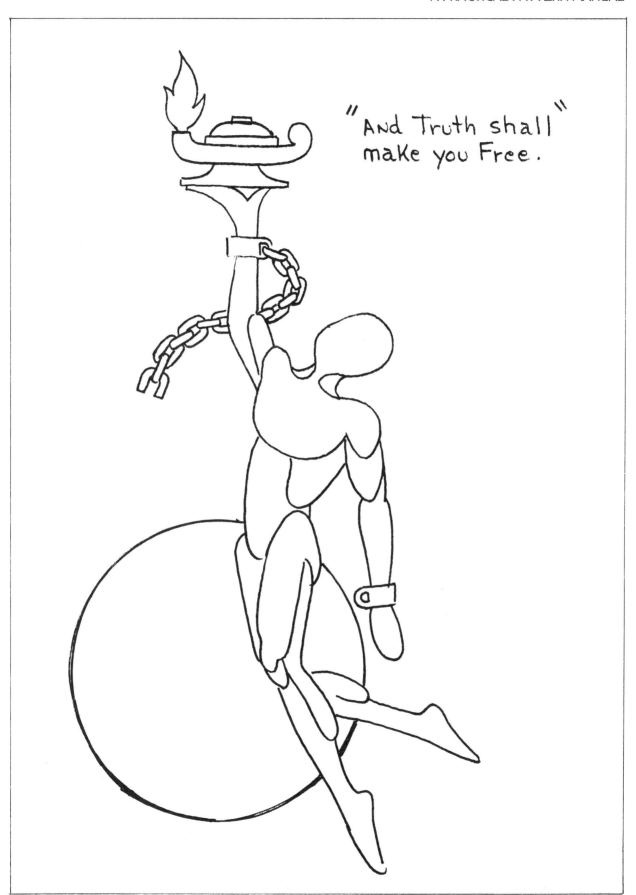

"And Truth shall"
make you Free.

Horse

I. Throughout history mankind has had a love affair with the horse, which has often been portrayed by artists. This version of mine is one of the simplest shallow relief carvings I could design.

II. Type of Carving

This is a cut-out relief carving, done in shallow relief with long, flat strokes.

III. Materials

    A. Tools

    1. V-Tools: ⅛″, ¼″, ½″
    2. Gouges: ¼″ #4, ½″ #4, ⅜″ #6
    3. Chisels: ½″ #1
    4. Knife
    5. Mallet
    6. Band saw or coping saw

    B. Wood
Basswood, mahogany, or walnut, 1″ × 9″ × 13″.

IV. Carving

    A. Transfer the design onto your board.
    B. Cut subject out of the board with the band saw or coping saw.
    C. Glue it down on plywood as was described for the Heavenly Kingdom carving.
    D. Strap the work down to a bench top.
    E. Use the ½″ V to outline the head and neck.
    F. Use the #4 gouge to remove waste on neck up to nose and jaw line to a depth of ½″. Round neck muscles slightly into crease lines of muscles.
    G. Leave nose top flat and gently slope carving back up forehead until the mane hair is reached between the ears. The hair should be raised out about ⅛″ from forehead. Slant carving line gently from ridge along nose to stop cut under jaw. Leave jaw raised up ⅛″ from neck muscles.
    H. The left eye is left untouched by these slanting cuts, then rounded

slightly to make it appear raised out. The muscles on the left side of the jaw can be put in with a ½″ V and the edge of the ½″ #4 used to slant the cut down smooth.

      I. Use the #6 gouge to gouge out ears.

      J. Reduce the level of the mane where it connects to the head and neck and let it flare out flush with the original surface and end of hair.

      K. The right eye and bridge of nose can be shaped with ¼″ V and small #4.

40

V. Finishing

      A. Sand down smooth with sandpaper. First use coarse paper, sanding with the grain, and then fine grit paper. Use a deer antler to compress the grain and polish the surface.

      B. Pry loose from retaining board.

      C. Stain with your choice of commercial stain.

      D. Finish with hand rubbed oil if hardwood, or commercial Deft in semi-gloss as a sealer if softwood. A neutral or clear shoe polish can be used after the oil stain on either hard or soft woods. Repeated coats, buffed with a shoe brush, will build up a good semi-gloss finish.

Music Composition

I. If you look closely at the photo and can read music you will see that this pattern comes from my carving called "Silent Night", for that is the music carved into the music sheet. Here the music is left off the pattern so that you may add any music desired. The bow to the violin was added to a second, more detailed, carving and I liked it so well that I decided to add it to this pattern as well.

43

II. Type of Carving

This is a cut-out bas relief carving.

III. Materials

A. Tools

1. V-Tools: ⅛", ¼", ½"
2. Gouges: ⅛" #5, ¼" #4, ½" #4, ⅜" #6, ¾" #5, ¼" #13, ⅜" #13, ¾" #13, 1/16 #8
3. Chisels: ½" #1, 1" #1
4. Knife
5. Mallet

B. Wood

Either basswood or julutong, 2" × 18" × 28", or 1" × 9" × 14", depending on the space available to you.

IV. Carving

A. Cut out the pattern on a bandsaw and use the method of gluing it to a board as described for the Heavenly Kingdom carving. Affix it to a work bench top.

B. Establish the highest points to be left at surface height before you recess any part of it. These points are:

1. The surface of the violin, particularly the bridge and strings.
2. The bridge and strings of the mandolin.
3. The black keys of the keyboard.
4. The roundels on the flute.
5. The middle and edges of the sheet music.
6. The upper left-hand tip of the bow.

All these points are at surface level, or just slightly below. The surface can be taken down gently with the #4 gouges.

C. Use the V tool to make your framing stop cuts around the violin and the top and bottom of the mandolin, excluding the right side that touches the flute. That portion must be set in with a shallower stop cut. Use the V around the tops of the instruments and to set in the center fold of the sheet music.

D. Use the gouges to relieve the waste wood around the instrument tops and smooth out the background with #4s.

E. Slant the surface of the mandolin down against the stop cut, framing the violin. Leave the bridge and strings raised.

44

F. Use a #4 or a chisel to round the string mass from bottom to top. Then use a small V-tool to put in each string very carefully. This is where the use of good, strong, straight-grained wood pays off.

G. Round the flute using a #4 or a chisel.

H. Use a small gouge to put holes in flute.

I. Slant the flared end of the flute and bottom of the violin, giving it the illusion of thickness; round the top of the flute bell.

J. You can round the wood portion of the bow by turning the chisel on edge and making a slanted series of cuts with the wing tips.

K. Use a ¼" V to separate the music sheets, after slanting the bottom angle.

L. The embossing on the mandolin can be put in with a ⅛" V, running very shallow, or with a knife tip.

V. Finishing

A. Sand smooth while still attached to the retaining board.

B. Pry loose and stain to suit.

C. Polish with neutral shoe polish or seal with a semi-gloss commercial sealer for luster.

Forest Clowns

I. Adventuresome, nosy, sometimes clumsy and full of young fun, these bear cubs are always into something, often with disastrous results. If they get too curious here, the result is predictable.

II. Type of Carving

Bas relief, but there are several ways of doing this one:

A. It can be laid out on a rectangular 2″ thick board and carved leaving the edges of the board to border the relief.

B. Use 1″ thick stock and cut the subject free from the background.

C. It can be converted to a design for a statue in the round.

The directions given here are for the first method.

III. Materials

A. Tools

1. V-Tools: ⅛″, ¼″, ½″
2. Gouges: ⅛″ #6, ¼″ #4, ½″ #4, ⅜″ #6, ⅜″ #11, ¾″ #13
3. Chisels: ¼″ #1, ½″ #1, or firmers of the same size
4. Knife
5. Mallet

B. Wood

Basswood, mahogany, julutong, pine or redwood, 1″ × 11″ × 14″ or 2″ × 22″ × 28″.

IV. Carving

A. First familiarize yourself with the masses as you draw your pattern. Note especially which of those masses overlap the others. In this manner, and this applies to all carvings, you will know the highest points which are to be left flush, or at surface level, and which points must be carved down to give the impression of being under or behind the upper masses.

B. Transfer your pattern to the wood and firmly strap your work down on a table or bench.

C. Alternate between your V-tools and your #11 gouge in setting stop cuts around the exterior of the entire subject. Use shallow stop cuts where the bears' bodies cross the tree. You do not want one standard depth on all stop cuts for that would set the tree at the same depth as the background.

D. Either draw a 1″ border around all four sides or keep an imaginary one in mind and use your larger gouges to start down in on a gentle slope to the stop cut. Your

#13 long bent will assist in removing waste wood up to the stop cuts. This process will give a border for your carving while leaving the subject raised out.

E. Reduce the tree down to your stop cuts around the bears. Gently round it so it does not appear flat. Do not make the rounding too pronounced, try to keep it flat enough to reflect the light. Leave the sections you wish to carve bark on slightly higher than the rest.

F. Utilize your stop-cutting tools on the edges of the limbs and heads of the bears to divide the body masses into sections. Do not make them all one depth. Ride in lightly in places like under the rear protruding leg of the top cub. Ride in deeper around the head of the lower cub since the forearm hanging onto the limb should appear further away from you, hence deeper.

G. Gently round the bodies to the stop cuts. Use your #4 tools to keep the strokes broad, flat and light reflecting. This way you can create the optical illusion of rounding without diving in too deeply at the edges. Note: if any of your figures in relief form take on the look of a bunch of sausages held together by a string try using a broad, flat surface stroke with a gentle slope towards the edges, then a pronounced slope when right at the edge. This will correct that kind of defect.

H. Gently hollow the cavities in the face. Where the eyes appear leave the nose as your highest point. Next hollow out the curved section of the jowl from the nose back to the eye hollow. Gently slope from the top of the eye hollow back towards the ears. These will be reset below surface level so that they appear to be at the back of the head. From the outer edge of the eye hollow slope the cut down towards the framing stop cut around the head. Leave a rim or slightly raised portion at this stop cut to indicate the jowl fur.

I. Slope the limbs so they appear to go under or behind the tree on the left side of the upper cub. Slope his right forepaw under his nose to the limb. On the bottom cub carve out the waste on his forearm that hangs from the limb. Slope his back down towards the stop cut, leaving the lower rim thick enough to set him off from the background. Just shallowly skim his lower leg, as it is a high point. Use a steeper tilt on your #4 (using wing tip) to set the angle cut between his left forearm and his rear leg as they encircle the tree.

J. Put in features with knife tip, ⅛″ V and round eyes with small gouge. Pupils can be set in with a nailset.

K. Gently skim the wasps' nest surface, slanting down abruptly at the edges. Ridges in the nest can be put in with ⅛″ #6 and #11.

L. Use your ⅛″ V to gently set in indications of hair mass. Directions are shown on pattern.

V. Finishing

A. Stain, wipe off excess and let dry.
B. Apply neutral color shoe polish, buff with a shoe brush.

The Hair
Shadowing is
only to show the
growth direction.
The outline is
needed, not shadow.

Grapes and Vines

I. Grapes and vines have been traditional carving motifs for centuries. These leaf patterns enhance many kinds of pieces, either in running border designs or in individual clusters. Bear in mind that nature never produces perfectly symmetrical forms, so each leaf or grape cluster varies, permitting the artist to expand or contract the design, according to his needs, without destroying the aesthetic nature of his composition.

II. Type of Carving

These are all relief carvings, done in either 1″ or 2″ thicknesses of wood.

III. Materials

A. Tools

These will vary considerably depending on the size you choose to do your carving. If you decide to enlarge the pattern choose larger size cutting sweeps to fit.

1. V-Tools: ⅛″, ¼″
2. Gouges: ⅜″ #38 (a back bent tool), ¼″ #4, ½″ #4, ¼″ #13, 1mm or 2mm #10
3. Chisels: ⅛″ #1, ¼″ #1
4. Knife
5. Mallet, for light use only, no major cuts on small work

B. Wood

Basswood, julutong or mahogany, 1″ × 11″ × 11″.

IV. Carving

A. Your stop cuts around the grapes and leaves will be made with gouges to fit curvature, and small V-tools and knife tip, with a straight down cut to desired depth. The small V-tools will provide stop cuts along the vines themselves.

B. Boost out waste stock to stop cuts. Use #13 or ⅛″ #1 to clean up tight areas. You may also lay the small V on its side and use that as a #1 to get in tight spots.

C. The leaf has raised sides and a recessed central vein. Put this and all vein lines in with small V-tools. The smaller #10 will make eye holes where leaves overlap.

D. Use small V-tools to shape individual grapes. Leave them fairly flat in the center to reflect light. Use the $^{\#}38$ backbent to slant down, shaping the finished grape. The small triangular pieces between each grape can be trimmed out with a $^{\#}1$, a firmer, or a knife tip.

E. The spiral creeper vines are shaped carefully with a knife, $^{\#}1$s and $^{\#}10$s. Round the mass to barrel shape, then use small tools to separate it into individual strands. Use small $^{\#}10$ to cut out circular hole in vine.

52

V. Finishing

A. Sand lightly, stain to desired color and buff with clear shoe polish.

Clusters of Grapes

No object in Nature is always balanced exactly the same on both sides.

Example of how Running Grape and Vines can form a border on a Carved Plate. Same design can be used straightened out as a border.

Clockmaker

I. This piece evokes the era of the old hand-crafts, when quality was the object of craftsmanship.

II. Type of carving

This is a bas relief which is cut free of the background.

III. Materials

A. Tools

1. V-Tools: ⅛″, ¼″, ½″
2. Gouges: ⅛″ #6, ⅜″ #6, ¾″ #6, ¼″ #4, ½″ #4, ⅜″ #8, ⅜″ #13, ⅝″ #13, ⅛″ #10
3. Chisels: ⅛″ #1, ¼″ #1, ½″ #1
4. Knife
5. Mallet
6. Cross-hatch wood stamp

B. Wood

Basswood, mahogany, julutong, pine or butternut, 2″ × 16″ × 26″.

IV. Carving

A. Note: when drawing up your pattern remember that this is a three level carving. The tall clock case is the most deeply recessed. The second level is the clockmaker and the work he is doing. The highest points are the table top, table facing, the bottom part of the table legs and the man's right foot.

B. Use your V-tools to make stop cuts separating the man from the background clock case. Remove waste with a large gouge.

C. Separate face, clock case and arm by stop cuts. Remove waste up under arm, leave blocked out mass for clock gears on table top. Remove waste over the arm up to the beard.

D. Nose and pipe are high points to use as a guide when carving face. Sink in eye hollows and hollow beneath nose. Slant head back with #4s from front cheek bones. Flatten cheek bones with #4.

E. Put in eyes with small tools and knife tip. The mouth is done the same way. Hair is put in with ⅛″ V-tool.

F. Clock case he is working on is at an angle. Slant front back towards his shoulder, and slant side of case back towards his fingers.

G. Slant table legs up towards a stop cut around table front. Embossing is done on the front of the table with small V and #10.

H. Stop cut across table leg bracing and remove stock to stool bottom. Reset legs and gradually work deeper, removing waste until you reach ground level of clock case front. Two front legs on stool are recessed slightly below bracing bar. Rear stool leg is recessed halfway to the ground.

56

I. Take off stool front with slight rounding so it fits the proper depth for the stool legs.

J. Recess the rear table leg so it appears out a short distance from the ground level.

K. Slant back across knees and thighs with a broad, flat stroke. Slant his right leg down slightly towards the foot that is forward. The front part of that foot has a flattened-off slant to indicate the sole of the shoe.

L. The cross bar on the table legs is set in a short distance.

M. Work in detail on clock parts and hands with small assorted Vs, gouges and knife tip to separate fingers, notches, etc.

N. Small tools also will work in all remaining detail of shirt, clock faces, etc.

V. Finishing

A. Sand smooth, compress detail with deer antler, stain and wipe, then let dry.

B. Polish with neutral shoe polish and buff with shoe brush.

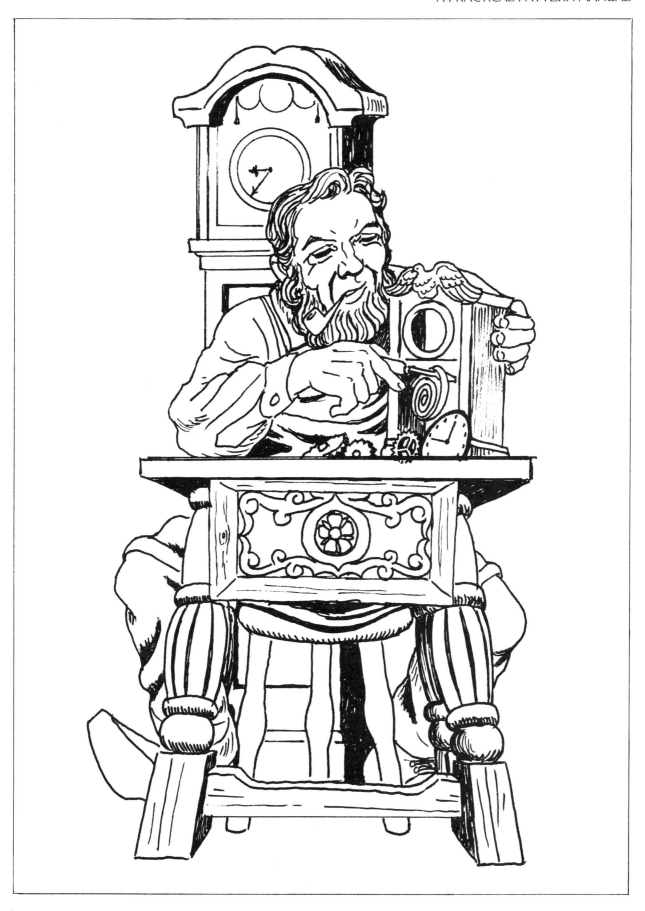

Roses

I. Floral patterns are always a challenge to carve since the leaves are so delicate, but they provide a wonderful motif and are highly satisfying once achieved.

II.Type of Carving

This is a bas relief carving, carved into a rectangular board, leaving a free form border.

III. Materials

A. Tools

1. V-Tools: ⅛″, ¼″, ½″ or ⅝″
2. Gouges: ⅛″ #5, ¼″ #5, ¾″ #6, ⅜″ #6, ¼″ #4 and ½″ #4
3. Chisels: ¼″, ½″
4. Knife
5. Mallet

B. Wood
Basswood or julutong, 1″ × 12″ × 16″.

IV. Carving

A. The first step is to understand your subject. In so doing you will immediately know which portions are high and which are low. The rose is really quite simple, it has a stem, on top of which is a button. The petals grow up and out of this in an overlapping, circular pattern. As the blossom opens the petals cease squeezing together and fall back loosely, but remain attached to the button. Your purpose is to carve the petals so that one overlaps the other, or to create the illusion that one goes down in behind the other. The petals have a tendency to come out and delicately fold over. You must undercut the edge slightly to give that fold-over effect.

B. Make your stop cuts along the edges of the petals with the V-tools. Use #4 gouges to slant down into the stop cut creating the effect that the petals grow out of a single stem. Use knife tip to cut under folded over petal and slant your gouge cuts back under to the undercut.

C. Gently round main swelling body of the flower. Do not round them at too pronounced an angle. Use the small V to shape the closed up petals in the crown. By turning the smaller #4 on edge and using the wing tip these smaller pieces of waste can be removed.

D. The stems are slightly rounded.

E. The leaves protrude from the stems. The veins on the leaves are put in with a small V and the edge of the leaf is "nicked" with the small V-tool to form small protrusions. Don't worry about these nicks being too pronounced or deep since the leaves look like a series of exaggerated points all the way around. The leaves are slanted in to appear as though they are behind the petals.

V. Finishing

60

A. Sand smooth, stain to the desired color and let dry.
B. Wax with neutral shoe polish, buff with a shoe brush.

Points
on
Leaf
edges.

Bacchus

I. This figure comes to us from ancient Greek and Roman times. Bacchus symbolized festivity and the bountiful gifts of nature with his hops for beer and grapes for wine, always triggers for merriment.

     The figure depicted is the young Bacchus astride a wine barrel, holding aloft a cup in one hand and grasping a baton crowned with grapes in the other. He is clothed in grape leaves, with a garland of grapes and leaves in his hair. The head of the adult Bacchus, adorned with traditional grape clusters and leaves, supports the wine keg. One might guess this to be his favorite position, for when the spigot is opened he need only jut out his lower lip to drink his fill.

II. Type of Carving

     A relief carving, cut free of the background.

III. Materials

     A. Tools

     1. V-Tools: ⅛″, ¼″, ½″

     2. Gouges: ⅛″ #6, ¼″ #4, ½″ #4, ⅝″ #4, ⅜″ #5, ½″ #6, ¾″ #5, ¼″ #13, ¾″ #13

     3. Chisels: ¼″, ½″

     4. Knife

     5. Mallet

     B. Wood

     Basswood or white pine, 1″ × 12″ × 28″.

IV. Carving

     A. Take careful note of the high points on the carving so you can determine which sections must overlap to appear in front, such as the baton in front of the face of the wine keg. Also, the spigot is out from the keg front. Since this is a 1″ carving all cuts will be of a flat, sloping nature, going down to the stop cuts without sharp diving in sharply.

     B. Cut out the pattern along exterior lines on a bandsaw or with an electric skill saw or a hand coping saw. Use a waste board to glue it down as described for the Heavenly Kingdom carving. This will permit you to clamp it down on a bench.

     C. Your stop cuts will mainly be set with the tip of the knife, and gouges that fit the curved sweep in places like the edge of the banner, around the cup, under the arm, along the hand on the baton and around the grapes and leaves on both figures.

D. Keep your gouge cuts to a flat shallow stroke. Do not attempt to dive in deeply. The banner which encircles the youngster is sunk down a little over ½", for example, as are the feet. You do not want to take them deeper in 1" wood.

E. The nose is the highest point on both faces, the rest slopes gently back under the hair and leaves. Due to the raised angle of the young head the lips and chin will be nearly as high as the tip of the nose.

64

F. The raised arm slopes back enough to appear as if the banner crosses over it, causing the hand to appear behind the cup.

G. The grape leaf waist band has each leaf overlapping slightly and rounds back to the rear near the sides.

H. Recess the keg end in flat, leaving the edge of the keg out, the spigot and baton raised from the ground.

I. Gently slope the angle from the nose back to the grapes on the adult figure. The bottom of the beard is flush with the surface. A hollow is created above the beard and under the nose. Hollows for the eyes are also shaped, leaving the forehead slightly raised. Features are put in with knife tip and ⅛" V-tool. Use the ⅛" gouge to refine detail around nose and eyes.

V. Finishing

A. Sand smooth. Use deer antler to compress grain and the tip of it to assist in smoothing the area around the eyes and nose and other hollowed-out areas.

B. Stain as desired, wipe and let dry.

C. Apply clear shoe polish and buff with a shoe brush.

Mare and Colt

I. For centuries mankind's development has been closely tied to that of the domesticated horse. Today, horses still hold a special fascination for people, even in urban areas where the inhabitants are exposed to horses only through riding stables, movies and television.

II. Type of Carving

A relatively shallow bas relief.

III. Materials

A. Tools

1. V-Tools: ⅛″, ¼″, ½″
2. Gouges: ⅛″ #6, ¼″ #4, ½″ #4, ⅜″ #6, ¾″ #5
3. Chisels: ¼″, ½″
4. Knife
5. Mallet

B. Wood

Basswood, 1″ × 11″ × 14″.

IV. Carving

A. Your first stop cut is with the ½″ V-tool from the tip of the mare's ears to the end of the tail. The second is from ears to nose. And the third is the jaw and neck line, followed by the forelegs. Use caution when you reach the colt's ears so that you do not break them off. Use short strokes in tight places.

B. Use the ¼″ V-tool to make a stop cut separating the colt from the side of the horse, and the rear of the mare's leg where it separates from the tail.

C. The ⅛″ V-tool is used for detail separation on the colt.

D. Boost out waste stock to stop cuts with ¾″ #5.

E. Use your #4 tools to shape the bodies. Use broad, flat strokes with a gentle sloping action to indicate flat surfaces, then a steeper slant near the outer edges to give a rounded look.

F. Manes and tails are detailed with ⅛″ V-tools, as are neck and jaw muscles. Grass is put in with both ¼″ and ⅛″ V-tools.

V. Finishing

    A. Sand smooth. Use deer antler to compress grain and accentuate muscles.

    B. Stain and wipe, let dry.

    C. Buff with clear shoe polish.

68

Keep muscle bulges shallow as there is no stress to cause deep bulging guts in this pose.

69

Bird in Grapes

I. This popular pastoral and romantic image is part of a design for a winery, the theme of which is nature and its bounty. The original is carved into a black walnut log which is the main support pillar in the building.

II. Type of Carving

This is a relief carving. To be effective it should be in high relief, that is, fairly thick to permit the bird to be handled in a realistic manner.

III. Materials

A. Tools
1. V-Tools: ⅛″, ¼″, ½″
2. Gouges: ⅛″ #6, ⅜″ #6, ¾″ #5 or 6, ¼″ #4, ½″ #4, ¾″ #4, ⅛″ #8, ⅜″ #8, ½″ #35, ⅜″ #35
3. Chisels or skew chisels: ⅛″ #1, ¼″ #1, ½″ #1
4. Knife
5. Mallet
6. Deer antler

B. Wood
Basswood or mahogany, 2″ × 14″ × 17″.

IV. Carving

A. Frame exterior of entire pattern with V-tool stop cuts and boost away waste stock.

B. The next stop cut is around the bird. Leaves and grapes will be flush high on exterior edges and cuts will slant down into these stop cuts, leaving the bird raised up and as the focal point.

C. Work in vine interior at upper right, remember that the leaf is behind the vine, so don't go in clear to the background level.

D. Set the level of the leaves at the upper right behind grapes and vine and boost out to the back of the bird.

E. Use back bend and gouges that fit the sweep to set in grapes. Clean up the triangular pieces left by your grape stop cuts with the tip of your knife or small chisels.

F. Set ground level of the leaves below vine near feet. Roll the leaves so that some surfaces are left high, while other areas go down and under.

G. Gently round the bird to shape. Use broad flat strokes rather than absolute rounding, a gentle sloping of the gouge until you reach the edge, then a steep downward cut.

       H. Now set in feather detail on the body with gouge tips, V-tools on tail feathers. Chisels to open mouth and small V-tools to open claws at feet.

       I. Small gouge will set in the eye and recess around the eye.

V. Finishing

       A. Sand smooth, compress the grain with the deer antler. Be sure to work the high surface of the grapes so they reflect the light.

       B. Stain as desired, wipe and let dry.

       C. Buff with clear shoe polish and a shoe brush.

Daisies

I. This particular design is derived from an appreciation carving given to me by a most gifted young Japanese carver, Mrs. Mioko Lewis of Missouri, who was a student of mine for a year or more. Her carving was a letter holder, with the same pattern carved on both sides. The delicate relief is raised out completely on one side, and recessed on the other, with the design carefully set down in without breaking off any protrusions around the tips of the flowers, a truly amazing display of skill. I keep the letter holder with pride and view it with fond memories of this talented woman.

II. Type of Carving

Relief carving.

III. Materials

A. Tools

1. V-Tools: ¼″, ⅛″, ½″
2. Gouges: ⅛″ #5, ¼″ #4, ½″ #4, ¾″ #4, ¼″ #13, ¾″ #5, ⅜″ #6, ¼″ #6
3. Chisels or skew chisels: ¼″, ½″
4. Knife
5. Mallet
6. Deer antler

B. Wood

Basswood, white pine, julutong or Japanese senwood, 1″ × 16″ × 13″.

IV. Carving

A. Set in stop cuts around exterior of the pattern with larger V-tool. Remove background waste up to stop cut.

B. Use smaller V-tool and set in the stop cut around the flower itself. Set in stop cut separating the leaves. The dark colored leaf edge indicates that it is rolled up. Make stop cut along the edge that is folded over nearly to the central vein. Shape the leaves, low at the center vein and rolled out higher, then slanted down towards edges.

C. Use ¼″ V to set in center button on flower. The knife tip or skew chisels can set in stop cuts around each petal, especially where they overlap, and will aid in removing waste stock. Keep the tips of the petals close to surface height, while sloping the petals back gently to the button.

D. Round the button slightly, leaving it raised a bit and set in cross-hatching with small V-tool.

E. The unopened blossom can be done with V-tools and #4s.

F. Round the stalk with #4 and knife.

G. Put the veins on the leaves with small V-tool or knife tip.

V. Finishing

A. Sand carving smooth. Apply vigorous pressure with antler to compress grain.

B. Stain desired color, wipe and let dry.

C. Apply clear shoe polish and buff with shoe brush.

X-Roll the
Leaf edge
up

Cowboy With Cup

I. This figure is typical of the Western cowboy. He is kneeling, drinking his coffee from a tin cup. A separate pattern of a campfire and coffee pot is provided so a set can be done.

II. Type of Carving

Bas relief cut free from the background.

III. Materials

A. Tools

1. V-Tools: ⅛″ ¼″, ½″
2. Gouges: ¼″ #4, ½″ #4, ⅛″ #6, ¾″ #6, ⅛″ #11, ¼″ #11, ⅜″ #11, ½″ #11, ⅝″ #11 (or similar sizes in 11 sweep), ⅜″ #13, ¾″ #13
3. Chisels: ¼″, ½″, 1″
4. Knife
5. Mallet
6. Deer antler

B. Wood
Basswood, 2″ × 22″ × 29″.

IV. Carving

A. Cut figure out with bandsaw. Laminate it to waste wood backing board.

B. Set in stop cut under hat brim and along neck and chin. Put in stop cut above the hat brim. Shape the crown mostly flat with steeply cut edges. Round the brim of the hat so it appears flat at the flared up side, then slants down in sharply at a steeply cut angle to the face.

C. Remember to keep the ear as the highest point when shaping the face. Keep the cheek bones up high also.

D. Stop cut from shoulder to elbow and elbow to coffee cup along arm. Stop cut under cup back along arm to where upper arm joins body. Set in stop cut with smaller tool around rolled up cuff.

E. Set stop cut from coffee cup over knee and set rolled up cuff.

F. Set in stop cut between right heel and left knee.

G. Set in stop cut along belt top.

H. Reduce level of right arm from surface level behind cup. Leave the forearm raised to surface level. Shape arm so as to leave a high point running from the middle knuckle to a point 1½″ in at rolled cuff. The mass of the hand slopes back from the middle knuckle to the left and from the forefinger knuckle to the right over the thumb.

    I. Skim the surface lightly, leaving most of the left arm as nearly flush with the surface as possible.

    J. Set depth of right thigh just below the surface and round deeper on the edges. Do the same with the right calf, setting it in behind the left knee at least 1¼″ deep.

    K. Sharply round the left thigh. Set in a stop cut back up under this thigh to set off lower leg and boot. Clean out body area behind left arm to a depth of 1½″.

    L. Clean out waste across shirt front from the crook of the left elbow across to the right shoulder which drops in behind the jaw and nose to at least 1¼″ depth. Be sure and leave stock to shape in shirt pocket flap.

    M. Round coffee cup slightly and do the same to the hand holding the cup. Use sharp cuts at a steep slant near outer edges along hand and arm.

V. Finishing

    A. Sand smooth and compress grain with the deer antler.
    B. Stain as desired, wipe and let dry.
    C. Finish with clear shoe polish and buff with a shoe brush.

VI. Add campfire and coffee pot.

Campfire And Coffee Pot

I. This is the companion piece to the wall hanging of the coffee drinking cowboy.

II. Type of Carving.

Bas relief cut free from the background.

III. Materials

A. Tools

1. V-Tools: ⅛″, ¼″, ½″
2. Gouges: ¼″ #4, ½″ #4, ¾″ #4, ¼″ #13, ⅜″ #11
3. Chisels: ¼″, ½″
4. Knife
5. Mallet
6. Cross-hatch wood stamp
7. Deer antler

B. Wood
Basswood, 1″ × 14″ × 17″.

IV. Carving

A. Cut out design and drill several holes between waste portions under lid lifter and between pot and handle.

B. Laminate it to a piece of waste board. Clamp board to bench.

C. Use ½″ V-tool to make stop cut along the top of the foremost rock. Shape each rock separately using V-tool and ¾″ #4.

D. Use ¼″ V to shape flames against pot.

E. Reduce pot down behind flames, rounding the pot shallowly.

F. Round top and cut waste clear in space where the lift is on top of the lid.

G. Cut the waste between the pot and handle out.

H. Use wood stamp on pot near flames to indicate fire-blackened pot metal. This stamp area will stain much darker than a smooth carved surface.

V. Finishing

A. Sand smooth and compress the grain with a deer antler.
B. Pry loose from backing board.
C. Stain to desired color, wipe and let dry.
D. Apply clear shoe polish and buff with a shoe brush.

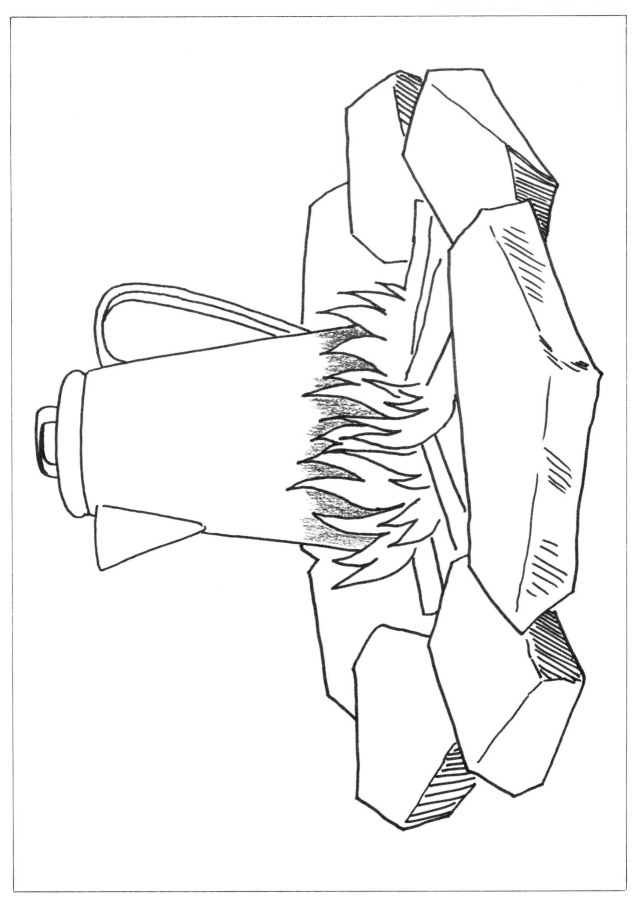

Wayside Philosopher

I. This my interpretation of a description of a German carving of an old gentleman, taking his ease against a fence and reading his favorite book. I drew him out on summer's day with his shoes off, his socks in his coat pocket and a sack lunch spread out on the ground near him while, like the boy he once was, his bare feet rest on a rock in the grass. I too would like to return to the peace of this setting and envy the "wayside philosopher" his total relaxation.

II. Type of Carving

Bas relief with a border.

III. Materials

A. Tools

1. V-Tools ⅛″, ¼″, ⅜″
2. Gouges: ⅛″ #4, ⅛″ #6, ¼″ #4, ½″ #4, ¾″ #4, ¼″ #13, ⅜″ #13
3. Chisels: ⅛″, ¼″
4. Knife
5. Deer antler

B. Wood

Basswood, 1″ × 14″ × 18½″.

IV. Carving

A. Set deepest portions down in. These are the sky behind the mountain top from face to right hand tree trunk. Set ground to full ½″ depth with #13s. The sky behind head and the space under arm resting on railing are not quite so deep.

B. Shape the head. Slant cheek bones away from the bridge of the nose. Left cheek slants off towards the background more steeply than the right. The beard and the hair strands are put in with a ⅛″ V (cut shallowly).

C. Use ¼″ V to make stop cuts separating the right hand and arm from the body.

D. Set the waste portions in between the rails to ¼″ deep. The mountain is thicker at the top, then merges down to the fence. Foothills show through the rails, but are carved in deeper than the mountain top. Tree trunks are recessed enough to appear to go behind the railings. Round the posts and railings slightly.

E. Use knife to put in stop cuts on body sections (see photograph). Do not round limbs too much nor put wrinkles in clothing too deep as you have limbs inside the clothing.

      F. Slant the foreground back from raised border to the legs, leaving all the objects in the foreground raised to surface level.

      G. Shape the objects.

V. Finishing

88

      A. Sand smooth. Compress grain with deep antler.

      B. Stain and wipe, let dry.

      C. Apply clear shoe polish and buff with a shoe brush.

Bald Eagle

I. To me this bird represents not only our country, but is also a symbol of fiercely independent freedom of spirit. Therefore I enjoy portraying him often, in this age of social and political pressure and upheaval.

II. Type of Carving

Bas relief cut free from the background.

III. Materials

A. Tools

1. V-Tools: ⅛″, ¼″, ½″
2. Gouges: ¼″ #4, ½″ #4, ⅛″ #6, ¾″ #6, ⅛″ #11, ⅝″ #11, ⅜″ #13, ¾″ #13
3. Chisels: ¼″, ½″
4. Knife
5. Mallet
6. Deer antler

B. Wood

Basswood, 2″ × 17″ × 26″.

IV. Carving

A. Cut out along the outside pattern line.

B. Set in stop cuts around the top of the folded wing, between wings at rear, under wing and behind leg.

C. Reduce the level of the rear wing. Slant cut in against stop cut in a broad flat sweep, then slant down sharply on outer edge.

D. Round the back at the point between the upper wings.

E. Reduce the level of the beak and set in detailing.

F. Slope the white feathers from shoulder up and around towards beak. You will reduce the stock considerably so that the upper plate above the eye is only slightly thicker than the beak.

G. Put in feathers around the eye with ¼″ V and ⅛″ #11. Round eye with ¼″ chisel.

H. Set ground level below foot.

I. Set level of tail feathers, slanted from high point at tips of tail feather up to stop cut under wings.

J. Shape foot and talons.

K. Round leg slightly.

L. Set in feather work, starting with the largest wing first, then back and rear wing. Continue on up to "bald" feathers. Do not put these in separately, use fold lines to create a smooth surface rather than individual feathers as these are long and wispy and adhere tightly to the head and neck.

M. Most of the feathers can be shaped with the ¼" V and the quills put in with the ⅛" V or #11.

92

V. Finishing

A. Sand smooth, compress grain with deer antler.

B. Stain to desired color, wipe and let dry.

C. Use white latex base or artist's paint on "bald" feathers on head and tail.

D. Use Deft sealer and steel wool in semi-gloss to seal stain and paint colors.

93

Continental Soldier

I. This figure is easily recognized by his costume, and the old original 13 star flag, as a soldier in our War of Independence. He stands at ease, but on guard for the rights of all.

II. Type of Carving

Bas relief cut free of the background, can be hung as is or mounted on the background of your choice.

III. Materials

A. Tools

1. V-Tools: ⅛″, ¼″
2. Gouges: ⅛″ #6, ⅛″ #11, ¼″ #4, ½″ #4, ⅜″ #13, ½″ #13
3. Chisels: ⅛″, ¼″, ½″
4. Knife
5. Mallet
6. Deer antler
7. Cross-hatch wood stamp

B. Wood
Basswood, 1″ × 7″ × 24″.

IV. Carving

A. Cut out design. Laminate to a piece of waste plywood. Clamp the board to work bench.

B. With knife and V-tools put in stop cuts along front of soldier to separate subject from flag background. Use #13 to set in ground level of the flag ⅜″ deep. At the bottom of the flag you will go clear through leaving the subject standing on a small plot which should be tooled to make it appear grassy.

C. Figure is tooled with broad flat strokes. Deep slanted strokes along the back will give a rounded effect.

D. Work face and hands in with smaller tools. Leave a higher ridge running down through the left cheekbone to the jaw. Slope face gently away from this higher line.

E. The stars in the flag as well as the braided tassles on the flag are detailed with the knife and ⅛″ V.

F. Darker stripes on the flag are cross-hatch stamping.

V. Finishing

    A. Sand lightly and compress grain with a deer antler.

    B. Stain to desired color, wipe and let dry.

    C. Buff with clear shoe polish and shoe brush.

96

Liberty

I. This portrayal of the American bald eagle and banner represents the origins of our country.

II. Type of Carving

Bas relief with the design raised from a "grounded" back board.

III. Materials

A. Tools

1. V-Tools: ⅛″, ¼″, ½″
2. Gouges: ⅛″ #6, ⅜″ #6, ¾″ #6, ¼″ #4, ½″ #4, ⅜″ #13, ½″ #13
3. Chisels: ⅛″, ¼″, ½″
4. Knife
5. Mallet
6. Deer antler

IV. Carving

A. Set in stop cuts along exterior lines of patterns.

B. Remove waste background leaving design raised up from ground.

C. Set in stop cuts both below neck and around leg and above neck.

D. Take down excess wood on wing to a depth of ¼″.

E. Take down tail feathers and slant down side of banner to tail feathers leaving roll of banner thicker.

F. Take down lower leg so that it is just thicker than lower wing.

G. Leave edge of upper wing flush, hollow out behind the high edge of the wing.

H. Put in feather detail with ⅛″ V and gouge tips.

I. Keep feather work to a minimum on the white head. Use a smooth flat stroke to keep it smooth.

J. Put in feet and talons with small V-tools.

K. Smooth down banner slightly below talons.

L. Use V-tools to letter in Liberty.

M. Use ⅜″ #6 in conjunction with other tools to clean out waste in folds of banner.

V. Finishing

    A. Sand lightly and compress those areas which need it with a deer antler.

    B. Stain as desired, wipe and let dry.
    C. Paint on white head, tail feathers and banner around letters.
    D. Buff with clear shoe polish.

100

Antique Auto

I. This '31 Auburn is one of America's classic cars from a long-gone era of splendor. The large sedans of that period represented an elegance and comfort which has never been replicated in the automobiles of today.

II. Type of Carving

Bas relief with a wide free-form border.

III. Materials

A. Tools

1. V-Tools: ⅛″, ¼″
2. Gouges: ¼″ #4, ½″ #4, ¼″ #13, ¾″ #6
3. Chisels: ¼″
4. Knife
5. Deer antler

B. Wood
Basswood, 1″ × 8″ × 15½″.

IV. Carving

A. Make a stop cut down in straight with knife around the outer edges of vehicle. Boost out waste border stock down to stop cuts.

B. Set in stop cut over fender wells and spare tire to set out widest points. Body will flare wide at the roof top and slant back in to meet the running board.

C. Set grill and spot lights back in, slant cuts back in shallowly, leaving horn and lights raised.

D. Slant off the hood, using knife tip or V-tool to put in trim.

E. Carve away what would be glass in a real car to show objects like the rearview mirror, steering wheel and seats raised at the same slant across the vehicle as the windshield frame top.

F. Work in under fenders setting tires out. Slant cut across front tread of tires. Leave wheel hub out flush, recess the area for wire spokes within the tire. V-shaped notching with a knife will create a wire wheel effect.

G. Shape the front bumper with a down and back in stroke, making it look like it tilts forward a bit at the top.

H. Roof slants across like the slant across the top of the hood.

V. Finishing

A. Sand lightly and compress the grain with a deer antler.

B. Stain as desired, wipe and let dry.

C. Buff with clear shoe polish and a shoe brush.

104

1931 AUBURN

105

Appendix
How to Use a Grid

108 How to use the transparent grid for enlarging a pattern

¼" squares

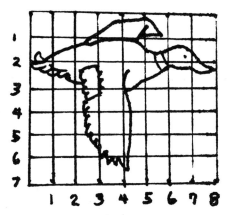

1. Choose your design and tape it down on table or board.

2. Lay grid over it so the squares cover it— in this example it is 8 squares wide and 6½ tall.

Enlarged to double size

3. Careful observation shows where lines of pattern cross the horizontal and vertical lines. By marking those spots, you can draw lines from one point to the next. You can enlarge to any size if you draw the squares to scale.

½" squares

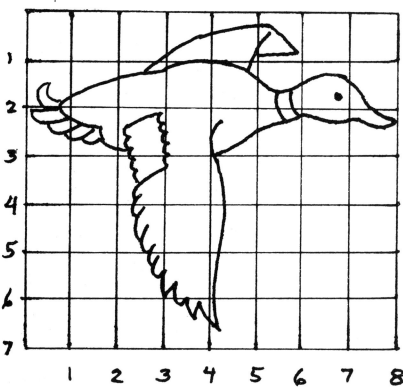

GRIDS
for copying and
enlarging patterns

A B C D E F G H I J K L M N O P Q R S T U V W

1
2
3
4
5
6
7
8
9